Augustus Goodyear Heaton

A Treatise on the Coinage of the United States Branch Mints

Augustus Goodyear Heaton

A Treatise on the Coinage of the United States Branch Mints

ISBN/EAN: 9783337340810

Printed in Europe, USA, Canada, Australia, Japan

Cover: Foto ©Suzi / pixelio.de

More available books at **www.hansebooks.com**

A TREATISE

ON

THE COINAGE

OF THE

UNITED STATES BRANCH MINTS,

A. G. HEATON,

Member of the American Numismatic Association.

WASHINGTON, D. C., 1893.

PRICE, ONE DOLLAR.

UNITED STATES MINTS.

THE PHILADELPHIA (PA.) MINT,

the principal or parent institution, was organized in 1793, and has coined all denominations of gold, silver and minor pieces from their authorization to the present, with but few interruptions. The minor pieces have never been struck elsewhere.

PHILADELPHIA COINS ARE UNMARKED.

THE BRANCH OR ASSOCIATE MINTS.

THE NEW ORLEANS (LA.) MINT

was organized in 1838, and from that date to 1861 coined, somewhat irregularly, all denominations of gold and silver pieces. In 1879 it resumed with Eagles and silver Dollars, and has since '92 coined Halves, Quarters and Dimes.

NEW ORLEANS COINS ARE MARKED WITH AN **O**.

THE DAHLONEGA (GA.) MINT

was organized in 1838 and suspended in 1861. It coined only gold pieces, Half Eagles and Quarter Eagles regularly, Dollars from 1849 to '61 and Three Dollars in '54 alone.

DAHLONEGA COINS ARE MARKED WITH A **D**.

THE CHARLOTTE (N. C.) MINT

was organized in 1838 and suspended in 1861. It coined only gold pieces, Half Eagles and Quarter Eagles almost regularly in the period named and Dollars almost regularly from 1849 to '59.

CHARLOTTE COINS ARE MARKED WITH A **C**.

THE SAN FRANCISCO (CAL.) MINT

was organized in 1854, and has since coined all denominations of gold and silver pieces, the former from Half Eagles upward regularly to the present, and silver regularly to 1878, when Dollars continued alone, with Dimes from 1884, until 1892 renewed Halves and Quarters also.

SAN FRANCISCO COINS ARE MARKED WITH AN **S**.

THE CARSON CITY (NEV.) MINT

was organized in 1870. Double Eagles, Eagles and Half Eagles were coined regularly from that date to 1884, as were silver Dollars, Halves, Quarters, Dimes, and a few Twenty Cent pieces were coined regularly to 1878. Since then very little has been done.

CARSON CITY COINS ARE MARKED WITH A **CC**.

PREFACE.

The coins of all other mints than that at Philadelphia are distinguished from its unmarked pieces and from each other by certain capital letters, indicating the city where they were struck, and are hence commonly known as 'Mint Marks.'

The writer, a few years since, after enriching his almost complete collection of silver and minor issues of the parent institution with all attainable varieties, became much interested in gathering United States coinage bearing the letters to which he has referred. The attraction of his pursuit grew with each piece acquired, each series completed, and each unknown variety found, until his modern dates quite divided his consideration with the old. The difficulties encountered were the lack of any guide-book to this new territory, the remoteness of the very few collectors who were also attracted to it, the absence of information among collectors at large, as well as dealers and experts, wise in older coinage, and consequently the entirely hap-hazard search for desired Mint Marks amid large stocks and private accumulations, because such pieces were not distinguished from similar Philadelphia dates, and saved in appreciation of a separate table of values.

The need of distinct estimates was evident. Preliminary searching proved that the rarity and consequent value of pieces of the same date from different mints were scarcely ever equal, and that some dates necessary to complete Branch Mint sequences never came to view.

The Mint Report, annually issued by the Government, was the first substantial ground of information.

Among its voluminous statistics are found lists of the coinage of every mint in the United States to the year preceding the publication of the Report with the not-always consecutive annual amount of the coinage of each denomination. This knowledge was valuable as indicating what dates a collector should look for, and what should be accounted scarce or rare from limited coinage.

But these statements had to be established by investigation and experience. It often happens that but a portion of the registered coinage of any piece is issued for circulation, the remainder being remelted. Occasionally an entire coinage has either never left the mint or has been sent abroad and recoined there. Thus the Report announces the coinage of several dates in different denominations never known to numismatists; but it omits also any reference to certain pieces which many collectors possess, and which are genuine and stubborn facts. The dates that exist in visible shape are, therefore, the essential things for a collector, and it became necessary in our new field of investigation to find out how far the Mint Report was realized in attainable coins.

Persistent attention and search brought their reward. Date after date was found, series after series completed, mintage after mintage classified until a collection was formed, from which we are now able to verify nearly every piece reported in the Branch Mints' coinage of silver from 1838 to the present year 1893. Of the total two hundred and seventy-seven dates, of all denominations, which these mints coined in the interval named, we lack but seven, and, knowing that three or four of these exist, have no doubt the remainder were coined also and will yet be found.

The unrealized dates of the Report are, therefore, confined to old Philadelphia coinage entirely, and the 'Mint Mark' field can no longer be avoided as indefinite and unsurveyed. The Mint Report is, indeed, only at fault in regard to Branch Mint coins from its omissions. No mention whatever is made of the existing Half Dime of 1838, the Quarter of 1849, and the Half Dollar of 1838 (all of the O mint), or of the excessively rare Dahlonega Mint gold Dollar of 1861.

With these exceptions the Report of our Branch Mint coinage gives the dates of each series accurately, and we are convinced, from an examination of large quantities of money in different sections of the country, that its statements of the amount of each date struck can be confidently taken as a basis for deciding relative or actual rarity, with due allowance for the unknown difference between coinage and issue, the location of the collector and other points referred to elsewhere.

As the Mint Report is not easily accessible to many collectors, we have digested all statistical information upon these topics of date and amount of coinage that could be of any value to them, and note in these pages the coins that are either scarce or rare from restricted number.

Here the usefulness of the Mint Report ends.

The VARIETIES of many dates are in no way referred to by it, though these are of the highest numismatic interest. We therefore have searched for and studied them with especial enthusiasm.

Some of these varieties are already known and have been described, but of more than an hundred recorded in this Treatise from examples in our possession, the greater portion are new to collectors and are now first published. They include large, small, and differently placed Mint Marks, high and low dates, broken dies, and other peculiarities which will give exceptional value to our lists beyond.

The estimates given of the rarity of these varieties, as well as of Mint Mark dates are the result of close attention to not only large quantities of money in circulation, but to the courteously submitted stocks of twenty coin dealers in various cities, whom we know personally, and our search has been so widespread, and the specimens seen and collected so sufficient for the purpose, that we feel assured the investigations of others will confirm all statements here made. Where a coin is not referred to as rare or scarce in these pages it should be understood to be of ample issue, and to be probably found without long search by any one having access to large amounts of money in prominent cities, especially those in the section where the coin is produced, but many more pieces would be scarce, of course, to a collector in a secluded place unfamiliar with bank tellers or trades' people. If, on the contrary, the chance of location enables a collector to find several coins of a date or variety we consider rare, he is the more fortunate, and will do well to preserve them. New varieties will, doubtless, be found from time to time as more active and general search is stimulated.

Such a search has only been delayed by the absence of exact lists of coins known to exist, close descriptions of them, and, in fact, some other information than that given in occasional catalogues of coin sales of stray Mint Mark pieces which the owner has usually acquired by chance on account of the date or condition alone.

This needed information, and our views at large upon the collection of Branch Mint coinage, we have decided to present publicly, as a cause of new interest in United States coinage at the beginning of its second century of existence, that others attracted to Mint Marks may better know what they require; that general attention may be given to a most fascinating branch of numismatic study, and that rare or scarce Branch Mint pieces may be sooner rescued from circulation and new varieties found.

May, 1893. A. G. H.

NOTE.

The Mints already mentioned, in the order of their organization after the Philadelphia Mint, were for many years strictly "Branch Mints" of the parent institution.

At present the direction of all mints of the United States is from a bureau in the Treasury Department at Washington, but as the older Mint still supplies the dies, issues the widest range of coinage, and is to be so enlarged as to have a capacity for any future demand, the term 'Branch Mint' may still, from a numismatic point of view, apply to the others, and, being the most concise designation available, is employed in the present treatise.

We have also, to avoid monotony of words, used the terms "coinage" and "issue" interchangeably where unimportant, having explained that all of a coinage may not necessarily be issued. The Mint Report gives the coinage only, the amount of issue being never published.

The mints furnish but the coins of the current year, whether the applicant be a banker or numismatist. Anterior dates can only be found in circulation or, of higher condition, in dealers' hands.

We have written this treatise upon Branch Mint coinage entirely from personal investigation upon the lines given in the preface, and have thus far seen or heard of nothing but fragmentary references to the subject in a printed shape, which have in no way added to information already acquired.

There may have been, however, in old catalogues or numismatic publications, which we have not chanced to meet with, lists of Branch Mint pieces, or well-studied articles covering, to some extent, the ground we have passed over, and even giving additional details.

If such exist we should be glad to know of them, and credit any knowledge they may give upon our subject, but as they have not been mentioned during our several years' interest in Mint Marks, we must consider any such articles as either very brief, very doubtful, or very inaccessible, and offer our researches as an original contribution at a time when some hand-book to this coinage is much needed.

Any information of the discovery of varieties of Mint Marks, not recorded in this Treatise, will be gladly received by the writer, and, if duly authenticated by inspection, will probably be published later in a supplementary sheet. Care should be taken that Mint Marks, flattened by wear, are not mistaken for varieties.

For the unacquainted reader it may be stated that the writer is not a Dealer. His artistic profession is better known to Philatalists than Numismatists from the reproduction of his painting at the U. S. Capitol, entitled 'The Recall of Columbus,' upon the 50-cent Columbus Stamp; but coin collecting with him is simply a relaxation from professional work, and, in common with all private collectors, he sells only occasional duplicates. Among these, however, are a number of Mint Marks accumulated for the study of varieties.

Persons requesting information should enclose the return postage to assure a reply.

This Treatise can be procured either through coin dealers and periodicals devoted to numismatics or directly from the author by sending the price in a money order, a postal note, or in a greenback so wrapped as to be unseen through the enclosing letter and envelope and at the sender's risk.

A. G. H.,

1618 17th Street, N. W., Washington, D. C.

THE COINAGE OF THE

UNITED STATES BRANCH MINTS,

OR SILVER AND GOLD PIECES,

COMMONLY CALLED

'MINT MARKS.'

THE NEED OF AMERICAN COLLECTORS.

The early coinage of the United States is very interesting to numismatists, both from its types and its varieties. Not only were the designs numerous, but the association of different 'obverses' and 'reverses,' the slight differences of the copies by different engravers of the same design, the overlooked blunders of many of these engravers, the letters and figures of different sizes, the overdating of coin of preceding years, the lettered or plain edges, the thick or thin planchets, and various other differences cause the existence of very many dissimilar pieces of the same date and value.

Over fifty varieties of the copper Cent of 1794 have been classified, and as many of the Half Dollar of 1795. The 1817 cent has nearly twenty dissimilar obverses, while, as all experienced collectors know, the number of early copper and silver United States coin that have approximately ten varieties, is too numerous to mention. The collection of these many varieties of the first fifty years of our coinage is thus very fascinating. But from the year 1840 the figure of a sitting woman, looking backward, seemed a good enough design for almost every thing in silver issues.

Taste and fastidiousness diminished, while mechanical methods of exactly reproducing and multiplying a die reached such perfection as to leave no appreciable difference between any two of a given date in thousands of pieces coined. For many persons the pleasure associated with the gathering of their early pieces has been succeeded merely by the slight interest of continuing their series, of having the later coins in 'proof,' or in possessing the very few of these which are really rare. Some well-meant attempts have, to be sure, been made in the new dies of 1892 and in the Columbian Half Dollar to awaken numismatic and artistic interest, but they greatly dispose the collector to slumber again until a worthy 'relief' is inspired.

We should on this centennial year of the first United States coinage (1893) advocate a return to the superb designs of our earliest dates were it not for the confusion which might result from much wear or from intentional alterations of the figures on modern pieces. Let us hope some imaginative brain and skillful hand may yet be authorized to produce new coins with the dignity, beauty, and simplicity of the old.

In the meantime there is a generally overlooked or neglected means of dispelling all apathy in connection with our modern coinage. There is a region of activity and study appreciated by a few which it is the object of this Treatise to open and map out that the many may hasten in to enjoy and possess its riches.

And this is the territory whose acres and quarter sections are now free.

The *collection of the coinage of the Branch Mints of the United States, in addition to that of Philadelphia, will not only sustain interest in the Nation's coinage as a whole, and especially in the issues of the last half century, but will be found worthy of the enthusiasm of both the young collector and the most advanced numismatist.*

The many causes of the attractiveness of the study and collection of 'Mint Marks' are given as follows:

CAUSES OF ATTRACTIVENESS.

1st. Mint Marks in their progressive issue at New Orleans, Dahlonega, Charlotte, San Francisco, and Carson City show the direction of our country's growth and its development of mineral wealth.

2d. Mint Marks in their amount of issue in varied years at different points offer the monetary pulse of our country to the student of finance.

3rd. The denominations of any one Branch Mint, in their irregular coinage and their relation to each other at certain periods, indicate curiously the particular needs of the given section of the land.

4th. A knowledge of the Branch Mint coinage is indispensable to an understanding of the greater or less coinage of the Philadelphia Mint and its consequent numismatic value.

5th. A knowledge of the coinage of the different Branch Mints gives to many usually considered common dates great rarity if certain Mint Marks are upon them.

6th. Mint-Mark study gives nicety of taste and makes a mixed set of pieces unendurable.

7th. Several dies were used at Branch Mints which never served in the Philadelphia coinage, and their impressions should no longer be collected as mere varieties.

8th. The very irregularity of dates in some denominations of Branch Mint issues is a pleasant exercise of memory and numismatic knowledge.

9th. This irregularity in date, and in the distribution of coinage, gives a collection in most cases but two or three, and rarely three or more contemporaneous pieces, and thus occasions no great expense.

10th. As the Branch Mints are so far apart their issues have the character of those of different nations, and tend to promote correspondence and exchange, both to secure common dates in fine condition and the rarities of each.

11th. The United States coinage has a unique interest in this production at places far apart of pieces of the same value and design with distinguishing letters upon them.

12th. As Mint Marks only occur in silver and gold coins they can be found oftener than coins of the baser metals in fine condition, and neither augment or involve a collection of the minor pieces.

13th. As Mint Marks have not heretofore been sought, or studied as they deserve, many varieties yet await in circulation the good fortune of collectors who cannot buy freely of coins more in demand, and who, in having access to large sums of money, may draw therefrom prizes impossible to seekers after older dates.

14th. The various sizes of the mint marks O, S, D, C, and CC, ranging from the capital letters of average book type to infinitesimal spots on the coin, as well as the varied location of these letters, defy any accusation of monotony, and are far more distinguishable than the characteristics of many classified varieties of old cents and 'colonials.'

15th. Mint Marks include noble enough game for the most advanced coin hunter, as their rarities are among the highest in value of United States coinage, and their varieties permit the gathering in some issues of as many as six different modern pieces of the same date.

16th. The face value of all the silver Mint Marks to 1893, being less than one hundred and fifty dollars, they are within the means of any collector, as, aside from the economy of those found in circulation, the premiums for rarities are yet below those on many coins of far inferior intrinsic worth.

17th. As the new Mint at Philadelphia will have a capacity equal to all existing United States Mints, it is probable that others will be greatly restricted or even abolished in no long time, and that Mint Marks will not only cease as an annual expense, but be a treasure in time to those who have the foresight to collect them now.

RARITY AND VALUE.

The value of a coin depends upon its rarity. Old coins have been reduced in number by many causes and made rare, even when the issue was large. But the influences of recoinage, export, loss by fire or flood, and excessive wear do not apply to modern pieces.

Mint Marks, therefore, depend primarily for rarity upon a known small coinage, or, what is practically the same, though not as evident, a partial issue only of the amount coined. This partial issue is more apt to occur with large silver pieces than small, as the full coinage of the latter is generally required.

If the coinage of given dates of Mint Mark pieces is not limited, their scarcity is influenced by many causes and uncertainties that do not apply to older American pieces now almost entirely in dealers' and collectors' hands. While loss of a portion of each year's coinage must be conceded even to modern pieces through restricted issue, export, and injury, other conditions than loss also govern Mint Marks more than Philadelphia coinage. The latter comes from one source, and can be gathered through regular channels, the former from many, which are very little known.

A collector in Philadelphia may have a fine set of that mint, and even of the O mint, and wait long before finding the majority of S mint pieces in circulation. One in Carson City may similarly, after gathering fine series of the CC and S mints, have his patience much tried in attempting to pick up a line of the O mint coinage of any series, although many of the dates exist, of course, in large numbers. Hence Mint Marks have an indirect rarity and value depending upon the location of the collector.

Yet, although he will usually collect the pieces of the nearest Mint in better condition than others, there are at times exceptional causes to the contrary, for when the banks of a community need subsidiary coin and the nearest Mint cannot supply it, shipments are made from a distant one, and the collector has unexpected opportunities.

CONDITION also affects the value of Mint Marks to a greater extent than of Philadelphia Mint issues. Though the Branch Mint coinage is all relatively modern, gradual circulation across the length and breadth of a continent causes most pieces to be much worn. We have been surprised at the low average condition of thousands of dollars' worth of coin which we have seen counted.

The lower denominations, the Dimes and Quarters, suffer particularly from their more common use, and but few Halves and Dollars are very fine. They serve a collector but temporarily, and, if a date of unusually rapid transfer from a distant section does not come to his view from time to time, he can only depend upon the uncertainty of correspondence to secure choice pieces by mail. He may find the coins of the nearest Branch Mint in high condition, but wait long to perfect his series of the others. Even the most accessible Mint Mark pieces are difficult to gather uncirculated. Hundreds of the Philadelphia issue have been for a long period saved annually in this condition, but very few coined elsewhere. We know, from prolonged visits to New Orleans and acquaintance with the very courteous officials of the Mint and sub-treasury there during the winters of 1892–'3, that about the only pieces of each year's coinage that escape circulation are the very few written for from a distance and those taken by visitors as keepsakes; but we were less surprised at this when we sought several months in vain for collectors in New Orleans and found no reputable coin dealers other than money brokers.

As to San Francisco, we know from correspondence that the coinage of the mint there has been very little collected, and is most difficult to procure of even a few years back in uncirculated condition. We have heard of no collectors in Carson City, Dahlonega, or Charlotte who might search current money or bank accumulations for the coins of these mints in past years.

Why is it that the South and the far West neglect such great numismatic opportunities? As a striking illustration of the result, we mention that the Twenty Cent piece was, in 1877, limited in coinage to but five hundred and ten 'Proofs' struck, of course, in Philadelphia. In 1876 there were ten thousand specimens of this coin struck at Carson City, yet, while any one can buy the proof of '77 for about three dollars, the '76 CC piece is excessively rare in any condition, and would, even if worn, command two or three times that price from a Mint-Mark collector. Therefore a series of Branch Mint dates is not only difficult to gather individually and collectively in any condition, but is especially so in the state numismatists most desire. There are, of course, some exceptions in dates of every denomination, which from very large issues are only of value when uncirculated, but in general the preceding statement holds. An uncirculated series is thus a worthy object of numismatic ambition, and choice Mint Marks will assuredly yet command far higher prices than the same dates from Philadelphia, or even than some of their own scarce pieces greatly worn.

Meanwhile Mint-Mark values must vary, more or less, with the growing demand, the supply discovered, the condition, the location of the collector, and the estimates of sellers and buyers in different sections of the country. As their number increases and the good judgment of dealers grows with daily observation of the supply and demand and the prices obtained at sales, we may expect to see the worth of each Branch Mint coin determined in given condition with something of the accuracy pertaining to the pieces issued at Philadelphia.

But existing rare dates of Mint Marks and uncirculated pieces should be searched for without delay that the supply may be known. Persons near the Branch Mints with access to large quantities of coin have a great opportunity for rich collection and very profitable exchange in this new field, and upon their activity partly the question of rarity and value for a while depends.

UNITED STATES SILVER MINT MARKS.

THE THREE CENT SILVER PIECE

Was issued at the New Orleans Mint in 1851 only. It is found in many collections as a variety, and is not rare, though having but an eighth of that first year's coinage in Philadelphia. The O is conspicuously placed within the points of the large C on the reverse.

THE HALF DIME.

This very interesting little coin, which was the first authorized by the United States Government, and coined at Philadelphia in 1792, is also in the front rank of Branch Mint issues. As such it was peculiarly the coin of the people, for in the extreme South and West no smaller denomination has ever been in use. It was struck in New Orleans, with a number of Dimes and a few specimen Half Dollars, in 1838 when that early Branch Mint was organized. The Half Dime coinage continued there annually until 1860, with the exception of the years 1843, '45, '46, and '47. The civil war then terminated the O mint coinage, but in 1863 the San Francisco Mint took its place and coined Half Dimes annually, with the exception of the year 1870, until 1873, when, as the nickel piece had proved more convenient, the coin was abolished. Its fixed limits and never-conflicting mint pieces add to the interest and economy of possessing a set, as no annual addition is involved. The O mint series numbers nineteen dates, but successive varieties found extend the writer's set to at least thirty-six.

THE O MINT HALF DIME COINAGE.

These pieces are as follows: 1838 (of which the issue is not recorded in the Mint Report) is without stars, with a large O in the wreath on the reverse, and is rare. There is also a variety with stars and a small o, which is very rare. 1839 is with stars (as are all to 1860), and has a small o. There are, apart from the perfect die, two varieties of broken dies. In one the break is from the elbow to the nearest star; in the other the break is on the reverse from the O of 'OF' to the L of 'HALF.' 1840 is found with and without the sleeve. The former has a small o, and is very rare; the latter has both the small o, which is rare, and the large O variety, which is very rare. 1841 has large O and small o varieties, both being scarce. 1842 has a small o only, and is very rare. There was no coinage in 1843. 1844 has a large O, which is very rare, and a small o, which is rare. In 1845, '46, and '47 there was no O mint coinage. 1848 has a large O and a small o, both rare. 1849 has a large O only, and is the rarest O mint half dime. 1850 has a large O and a small o, the latter being very rare. 1851 has a large O. 1852 has the same only, and is very rare. The large O continues in 1853, of which date there are two varieties, one with arrows, being common, and one without, rare. There is also an exceedingly rare variety with a broken die, which gives the date the appearance of being over '51. 1854 has a large O, which is sometimes close to the letters and sometimes to the bow-knot. It is a common enough date. 1855 has a large O, and is scarce. 1856 has a large O, and high and low date varieties. 1857 has a high oval O and a low round o. 1858 has a large O, and the ribbon and stem at right touching in one variety and well apart in another. 1859 has a large O with high and low varieties, both being scarce. 1860 is without stars, the legend replacing them, and has a different wreath on the reverse. The o is small, and, for the first time, is under the wreath instead of within it. There are high O and low o varieties.

We have also two worn specimens of 1837 without stars, and sufficient traces of a small o in the proper place to convince us that some Half Dimes were coined experimentally in New Orleans in that year with a die similar to the one then used in Philadelphia, although the New Orleans Mint was not regularly organized until 1838. As the coinage of Half Dimes at New Orleans in the latter year was not recorded, though well known, we are the more assured of the authenticity of our '37 O mint pieces which were found in New Orleans, and we consider them excessively rare.

While the half dimes of '37, without stars, was coined in Philadelphia that variety of '38 was issued only at New Orleans, all struck at the parent mint having stars. The rare O mint dates we review in order, 1849, '44, '42, '52, '38, and '48, the rarest first.

THE S MINT HALF DIME COINAGE

Bears a very small Mint Mark, which, with one exception, is under the wreath. The dies of the coin are those of the same date of the New Orleans and Philadelphia Mints, a seated Liberty surrounded by "United States of America" and a wreath of wheat, &c., on the reverse.

The first five dates, 1863, '64, '65, '66, 'and '67, were of small coinage, and are scarcer than most of the preceding O dates, but by no means as rare as the similar Philadelphia dates, whose places they generally hold in collections. 1884 is the scarcest of the five, followed by '83. 1868 and '69 are more common. In 1870 no Half Dimes were coined in San Francisco. 1871 is the only date with the S within the wreath, and is exceedingly scarce. 1872 and '73 have the S below as usual, and the latter is somewhat scarce. We have discovered no varieties in the S mint coinage, our set thus numbering ten pieces.

Since the Half Dime was abolished in 1873 the inconvenience of the small piece has resulted in the annual remittance to the Treasury and the Mints of hundreds of dollars worth which street car companies, etc., are glad to have destroyed. Consequently very few Half Dimes now exist in circulation; their general scarcity and rarity is augmenting, and the small space a collection occupies will assure them ever increasing favor.

THE DIME

Has been coined at New Orleans, San Francisco, and Carson City.

THE O MINT DIME COINAGE

Has several sizes of the indicative letter which may be classified in three: the *large*, which is about the height of the letters of the legend "UNITED STATES OF AMERICA" on the coin, the *medium*, about two-thirds, and the *small*, about one-half or rather less.

The complete series of dates and the varieties found are as follows:

1838, the first date coined, is a piece without stars or legend around the seated Liberty on the obverse, and with a large O under "ONE DIME," and within the wreath on the reverse. It is quite scarce. 1839 has thirteen stars around the figure on the obverse, which continue until noted beyond. The reverse is in general the same as '38, but offers two varieties, a medium and a small o. 1840, which we have seen 'without drapery' only, has also two varieties, a large O and a small o. 1841 has a small o. 1842 has a small o. 1843 has a small o, and is quite scarce. There was no coinage in 1844. 1845 has a large O, and is scarce. In 1846, '47, and '48 there were no Dimes coined at New Orleans. 1849 has two varieties, a large O and a small o, and is somewhat scarce. 1850 has a large O and a small o. 1851 has a large O. 1852 has a large O. 1853 has a large O, and is the first Dime with arrowheads. We have seen no variety of 1853 O without. 1854 has a large O and arrowheads. There was no coinage in 1855. 1856 has a large O and a medium o, and the arrows are abandoned. We have also a large O variety with the legend so faintly struck as to be hardly perceptible. The large date '56 is found only in Philadelphia coinage. 1857 has a large O. 1858 has a large O, and is scarce. 1859 has a large O and a medium o placed lower than usual. In 1860 the stars give place to the legend, and on the reverse the o is very small, and for the first time appears under the changed wreath, as in the Half Dime of the same date. The 1860 O Dimes is of very small issue, exceedingly rare, and a great prize.

At this period the civil war occasioned a long interval in O mint coinage, and not until 1891 were Dimes again struck. The piece of that date resumes the design of 1860 on obverse and reverse, but has a medium o under the wreath in two varieties, one well centered and one close to right ribbon. In 1892 the seated Liberty is replaced by a wreathed head facing to the right, and the wreath on the reverse is changed in various slight details. The O continues of medium size under the wreath. 1893 is similar in all respects to 1892

The years of no coinage being 1844, '46, '47, '48, and '55, five in all, it will be seen that the dates of the O series from 1838 to '93, inclusive, number twenty-one, to which the addition of seven varities named make twenty-eight as the complete set. The smaller o of six of these varieties is uniformly rarer than the large one.

THE S MINT DIME COINAGE.

The mint mark letter S identifying this series may also, as in the preceding, be divided into three sizes: The *large*, being somewhat larger than the letters of the legend, the *medium*, somewhat smaller, and the *small*, about half their height and quite minute.

1856 is the first date of this series, the date being always small. Stars surround the seated Liberty, the obverse and reverse dies being similar to the O mintage of the same period. The S is large and in the wreath. The piece is rare. No 1857 Dime was coined at San Francisco. 1858 has a medium s, and in other respects is similar. It is rare. 1859 has a medium s, and is also rare. 1860 is especially interesting from continuing the stars when the O and P coinages of this date had discarded them. A medium s remains within the wreath. It is scarce. In 1861 the new dies, with a legend around the figure and the wreath of oak and wheat, were used. A small s first appears and is placed under the wreath. 1862 is the same. 1863 continues these characteristics, and is rather scarce, but the Philadelphia dates from '63 to '67 are all far rarer than the S coinage. 1864 S is like '63, and is comparatively common. 1865 continues the small s below the wreath, as does 1866. The latter is scarce. 1867 is scarce also and similar in detail, except the S is not quite so small. 1868 and 1869, however, continue the minute s. 1870 is unchanged, but a small coinage makes it very rare. 1871 is abundant. 1872 is rather scarce. 1873 introduces arrows for the first time at each side of the date. The variety without does not seem to exist in the S coinage. 1874 continues the arrowheads and the small s. 1875 omits the arrowheads. It has two varieties, a medium s within the wreath in one, the usual small s below in the other. In 1876 the latter only has been found. In 1877 also.

A long break in the sequence of the San Francisco coinage then occurs, but in 1884 the same design and the small s under the wreath are maintained. It and the five preceding dates are all very abundant, but in 1885 the smallest issue of the whole series makes that piece very rare. The S is almost medium in size. This somewhat larger S than usual under the wreath continues in the ample coinage of 1886 and the very large ones of 1887 and 1888. 1889 has two varieties, a medium s and a small scarce s. In 1890 the S is larger. 1891 presents it small. In 1892 and '93 it is nearly of medium size, still under the somewhat varied wreath. The obverse of this date gives the new design of a garlanded bust turned to the right, and the date is smaller than any preceding it except 1856. None of these dates are scarce after '85.

In reviewing the S series it will be seen that the years of no coinage were 1857 and from 1878 to '83. The rarities are, in order of importance, 1885, '70, '58, '59, and '56. 1866, '60, '67, and '63 are rather scarce. The dates and varieties mentioned number thirty-three, to and including 1893.

THE CC MINT DIME COINAGE

Is recognized by two very small c's, smaller than the small s of the last series, and they do not vary perceptibly throughout the eight dates of this mint issued.

The first Dime of Carson City is that of 1871, with the seated Liberty surrounded by "UNITED STATES OF AMERICA," on the obverse, as in the P and S coinage of the same year, and the wreath of wheat, corn, oak, &c., on the reverse. This piece and the three succeeding dates are all very rare. The CC are close together and under the wreath in these. 1872 is the second date. 1873 we know of without the arrow-heads only. 1874 is the highest rarity of the four.

We have 1875 in three varieties: The first has a close CC below the wreath, the second has a close CC within the wreath, and the third has a wide C C within the wreath, the latter two very scarce. 1876 has the usual close CC under the wreath. 1877 repeats this, and has a variety, with the CC a trifle larger. 1878 continues the close CC. It is somewhat scarce, but the three dates before it very common.

The Dime has not been coined at the Carson City Mint since 1878, and probably will not be in future.

COMPARATIVE TABLE.

The issues of the three Branch Mints named are associated with the Philadelphia dates of dimes in the following interesting list:

1838, P. O; 1839, P. O; 1840, P. O; 1841, P. O; 1842, P. O; 1843, P. O; 1844, P; 1845, P O; 1846, P; 1847, P; 1848, P; 1849, P. O; 1850, P. O; 1851, P. O; 1852, P. O; 1853, P O; 1854, P. O; 1855, P; 1856, P. O S; 1857, P. O; 1858, P. O. S; 1859, P. O. S; 1860, P. O. S; 1861, P. S; 1862, P. S; 1863, P. S; 1864, P. S; 1865, P. S; 1866, P. S; 1867, P. S; 1868, P. S; 1869, P. S; 1870, P. S; 1871, P.S. CC; 1872, P. S. CC; 1873, P. S. CC; 1874, P. S. CC; 1875, P. S. CC; 1876, P. S. CC; 1877, P. S. CC; 1878, P. CC; 1879, P; 1880, P; 1881, P; 1882, P; 1883, P; 1884, P. S; 1885, P. S; 1886, P. S; 1887, P. S; 1888, P. S; 1889, P. S; 1890, P. S; 1891, P. S. O; 1892, P. S. O; 1893, P. S. O.

No date has more than three pieces, and it will be seen that the collector triplicates his dates in but fourteen years of the fifty-five from 1838 to '93. He doubles them only in thirty-one years, and in ten the Philadelphia pieces stand alone. Thus Mint Marks are not, after all, such a great extravagance.

THE TWENTY CENT PIECE,

Like the silver Three Cent and the gold Three Dollar coins, has but very little for the interest of the Mint-Mark collector except in one rarity.

The Philadelphia Mint issues of 1875, '76, '77, and '78 complete that series. The coinage of every date was small, especially the latter two, which were in 'proof' only. The only S Mint piece, 1875, has a small s directly over the Y. There were coined considerably over one million of these pieces, or nearly six times the amount of all other coinage of them. The Carson City Mint coined a moderate quantity in 1875 with the C C wide apart, one over the Y the other over the "c" of 'CENTS;' also a small quantity in 1876 The pieces of 1876 CC have become very rare, as we have mentioned in our preface, from the negligence of Western collectors, or the indifference of all to Mint Mark rarities while the proofs of '78 (coined in Philadelphia to but about a twentieth of the amount), can at any time be bought. Thus the twenty cent piece has but three Mint Mark dates one being a prize We have not remarked any varieties.

THE QUARTER DOLLAR

Has been coined at New Orleans, San Francisco, and Carson City.

THE O MINT QUARTER DOLLAR COINAGE

Began in 1840, and, excepting the years 1845, '46, and '48, continued to 1860. After a long interval, begun by the civil war, it was resumed in 1891, and continued with the new bust of Liberty design in 1892 and '93. The coinage of the existing O mint quarter of 1849 is not recorded in the Mint Report. The scarcer dates are 1851, '52, '91, and '55. The Mint-Mark letter may be classified in this series as of three sizes, a large, a medium, and a small. The large is nearly as large as the letters of the legend, the medium about two-thirds, the small about one-half the height of these letters. The complete set of dates and a few varieties we have found are here described: 1840 has a small date and well-known varieties with and without a sleeve, the latter being apparently peculiar to this mint. The sleeve variety has a *medium* o over the " R " of QUAR., and by the point of the left stem, the other a large O over the space to the right of the " R," and evenly placed between the stems. 1841 has also a small date and two varieties of the medium sized o, one being over the " R " and the other over the space to the right, as before. 1842 has a large date and the medium o over the space. In the O mint it is as easy to get as the preceding, but is very rare in the Philadelphia coinage, and most collectors will find themselves depending on a Mint Mark for this date. 1843 has a small o over the space and a large date. 1844 has a medium o over the space.

There was no coinage, it will be remembered, in 1845 and '46. In 1847 the date is very large, and the medium o is over the space. 1848 continues the size of the date and O of the last piece, but the O is high between the stems. In 1849, a piece only scarce, there was no coinage recorded in the O Mint Report, but neither this piece or others in the '40's have the scarcity of similar Philadelphia dates. 1850 has a medium o close to the right stem and an upright 5 in date, unusual in the '50's. 1851 has a large O close to the left stem, and is the scarcest piece of the series, though not strictly rare. 1852 is quite scarce. It presents a large O close between the stems and over the space. 1853 appears with arrowheads and the rays, used only in this year's issue. It is quite common. If the rare variety without arrows and rays exists in O coinage we have not yet heard of it.

There are two varieties as regards the location of the large O mint mark, one is well centered over the space, the other is close to the notch of the stems 1854 has arrowheads only and the large O in two varieties, one well centered over the space, the other broadly restruck, and touching the R on the upper right curve. 1855 has a large O over the R, and is rather scarce. 1856 has an upright 5 in the large date and a large O over the space. The arrowheads cease. 1857 presents a large date and a large O high above the R and between the stems. 1858 has the O lower, but is otherwise similar, except in an upright 5 in the large date. 1859 has a small date and a well-centered large O. 1860 shows the same details. An interval then extends to 1891. This piece unchanged in design, has a medium date and a small o between the stems high over the right side of the R. It will be rather scarce. 1892 offers the new dies of a garlanded bust facing right and an heraldic eagle on the reverse. The date is of medium size and the Mint Mark is an exceedingly small o, just under the middle of the tail and over the R. 1893 continues the new design. This series numbers twenty-one dates to 1863, and a few varieties which can doubtless be increased.

THE S MINT QUARTER DOLLAR COINAGE

Began in San Francisco in 1855, fifteen years after the first O date, and, with the exception of the years 1863, '70, '79 to '87, inclusive, '89 and '90, have been struck annually to the present year.

A very interesting feature of this series is the large size of the Mint Mark on the earlier dates. The "S" exceeds in proportions those of the word "STATES." There are at least three other sizes on later dates, which may be called *medium*, *small*, and *very small*, ranging from within the height of letters of the legend to hardly more than a dot. They are invariably under the eagle on the reverse. There are twenty-six dates of this series to 1893 and a few varieties. We describe in detail the set we have thus far gathered.

The 1855 has slanting fives, arrow heads, and a large S high over the space to the right of the R. The 1856 has an upright 5, no arrows, a large high date and a large S high over the R. It has also a variety with the S high over the space. 1857 has a large date and a large S highly placed almost over the space. It is not common. 1858 continues the upright 5 and large date. A large S is high over the space. 1859 commences the small dates and has a large S nearly over the space. It is not common. 1860 presents a small date and a large S high over the space. It is a scarce piece. 1861 continues the small date. The large S is well centered over the space. 1862 only varies in the large S being high over the space. It is somewhat scarce. There was no coinage in 1863. 1864 has a medium date and a large S high over the space. It is the date of smallest coinage in the S series and is very rare. 1865 continues the medium date that rules hereafter. It has a large S high over the space and is scarce. 1866 is the first of the series with the motto "In God We Trust." It is also the first to dismiss the large mint mark and show a very small s that continues with little change through the rest of the San Francisco Quarters. The S in this date is close to the point of the left stem and over the R to the left. The piece is very rare, ranking next to '64. In 1866, for the first time, the Philadelphia quarter has a smaller coinage and so continues for the next three years, but could be more readily found especially in fine condition. 1867 repeats the details of the preceding date. We have found it also very rare. 1868 and 1869 have the same appearance but are not scarce. There was no coinage in 1870. In 1871 the small s crowds upon the point of the left stem. The piece is very rare. 1872 has the S midway between the left stem and the R. 1873 we have found only with the arrow heads which had been omitted since 1855. The s is smaller than before—the very small size—and is well centered between the stems, nearly over the space. 1874 again omits the arrow heads and has the same details regarding the Mint Mark as the preceding date. Of 1875 the same may be observed. 1876 shows two varieties, one with the very small s nearly over the space and the other with a medium small s over the R. 1877 also has two varieties—a small s close above the R and a medium small s highly placed nearly over the space. 1878 has a medium small s well centered nearly over the space. All these dates after '71 should be readily found—1874 to 77 being especially abundant.

An interval of coinage then occurs until 1888 when there was another great issue which should be distinguished from the very rare Philadelphia piece of this date.

The 1888 S has a medium small Mint Mark well centered nearly over the space. 1891 was the next year of coinage and will be rather scarce. There are two varieties. In one the medium small s is rather high and almost over the space, in the other it is centered over the R. In 1892 the new designs of a garlanded bust, facing right on the obverse and an heraldic eagle on the reverse side appeared on the San Francisco coinage simultaneously with that at New Orleans and Philadelphia. The S Mint Mark is exceedingly small. It touches the middle of the eagles tail and is just over the R. 1893 we have not yet received.

This list gives a total in dates and varieties of thirty pieces for the S mint series from 1855 to '93. We review the rarest dates as those of 1864, '66, '71 and '67, and the scarce ones of the years 1860 and 1865.

THE CC MINT COINAGE OF QUARTER DOLLARS

Extended from 1870 to 1878 with the exception of the year 1874, so that there are eight dates in this interesting series, the first four being of very small coinage. 1870 has a medium date and a widely spaced small c c over the letters A and R of QUAR. It has the smallest coinage of the series, and is exceedingly rare. 1871 has the same details and is also exceedingly rare. Of 1872 the same may be said, and in rarity it ranks next to 1870. 1873 has the same details and two varieties, one with arrow heads to the date and the other without. Both are exceedingly rare. 1875 has a large date and a close cc over the R and the space to the right. It is not common. 1876 has a large date, and two varieties—the close small cc high over the R and a slightly larger cc, not so high. 1877 has a small date and a close small cc over the R. 1878 has a small date and a close relatively large CC over the R and partly over the space. The latter three dates were coined in immense quantities.

The largest size of the very little varying Mint Mark of this series is very small in comparison with that of other mints, for it was used after the obtrusive Mint Marks of the early dates, especially the San Francisco pieces, had yielded to an evidently general policy of making them merely sufficient for identification if necessary.

The three Branch Mintages of Quarters conflict very little. The O Mint issues are alone from 1840 to '54. From '55 to '60 there are O and S Mints. The S series then runs alone to '69. From '70 to '78 with one exception in each mintage, it has the CC dates in its company. Then, except a single S Mint coinage in '88, there is a break to 1891, when the O and S Mints resume, and have since continued.

THE HALF DOLLAR

Has been coined at the Mints of New Orleans, San Francisco and Carson City. These Mintages are related to each other very much as are the Quarters to which we have just referred. The O dates run alone from 1838 to 1854. From 1855 to '61 the O and S pieces are contemporary. The S series then continues alone until 1870, when the Carson City coinage starts in and accompanies it to 1878. Then all Branch Mint coinage of Half Dollars ceases until 1892, when at San Francisco and New Orleans they are struck with the new dies.

It will be remarked that, up to the latter year, there are only seventeen doubled pieces to be added to the Philadelphia dates in a period of fifty-five years. The collector, therefore, who, without investigation, has fancied that he would need to buy perhaps three Mint Mark pieces for each year of the half century, may be much reassured.

THE O MINT COINAGE OF HALF DOLLARS

Commences in 1838. There is no record of that year in the Mint Report, and probably only a few specimen pieces were struck, as less than a dozen are now known, and they are not merely among the rarest Mint Marks, but the rarest pieces of United States coinage. The value this high Mint Mark rarity has acquired augurs well for others when the whole subject is more familiar to collectors. The 1838 Half Dollar has a medium sized o on the *obverse* of the piece and beneath the bust of that year. 1839 retains the O under the bust facing left on the obverse. The piece has a large date and is not common. In 1840 the dies of the Half Dollar were changed, and the seated Liberty and spread eagle continued long afterwards. The date is small, and an O of the large size is under the eagle, on the reverse (as always since), and just over the 'F' of the word HALF.

There is a variety of this date with a very small o mid-high over the F. There is no other small o until '92, and what we have termed the large size is not much more than half the height of the letters on the reverse. 1841 has a small date and a well-centered large O over the F. 1842 shows a large date and a large O mid-high over the F in one variety, and over the space between L and F in another. 1843 has the large date, which so continues as not to need further reference, and a large O somewhat to the right, over the F. 1844 has two varieties, a large O, rather high over the F, and a medium sized o placed lower. There is also a curious restrike of this O mint date. 1845 has an upright 5 and a medium o mid-high over the F. 1846 resumes the large O, which is high over the F. 1847 is similar. 1848 only varies in that the O about touches the stem above. 1849 has also a large, very high O directly over the F. We find 1850 the same, and 1851. None of these dates from '39 down can be called scarce. 1852, however, claims that distinction. It resembles the two or three preceding pieces. 1853 appears, as at Philadelphia, with arrowheads for the first time, and rays on the reverse for the only time The O is large. This piece is common, but, if the judgment of several authorities is well founded, there is a variety of the 1853 O mint without arrows and rays similar to the Quarter of the Philadelphia Mint, but never known in the Half Dollar coinage of that institution, which takes at a bound the highest place among Mint Mark rarities. Such a piece has been purchased as genuine for considerably over one hundred dollars. It was found in the West. We are disposed to recognize the possibility of such a variety, but, as we have seen the usual pieces with the rays and arrows so skillfully removed as to 'deceive the very elect,' we warn collectors to be very much on their guard. 1854 continues the arrowheads, and has a large O mid-high over the F in one variety, while in another it is nearly over the space and close to the stem. 1855, with arrowheads also, shows the usual Mint-Mark high over the F.

In 1856 the arrowheads disappear for good. The large O is so high over the F as nearly to touch the stem. Besides the 'perfect date' of this piece we have two restrikes, one below the figures and one above. Whether from a defective machine or unskilled workman the frequent 1856 restruck dates are usually of the O mint. The 1857 piece has the O close to the stem also, and rather to the right of the F. 1858 and 1859 present the same details. In 1860 the O is merged with the stem above the F. 1861 shows the mint mark nearly touching the stem, above the F also.

After a long interval the Half Dollar was struck in 1892 with the new bust and heraldic eagle dies. The date is small, and a small o is directly under the middle of the eagle's tail and over the D. There is one rare variety of this piece with an exceedingly small o, hardly larger than a period.

The 1893 as far as we have seen, resembles the usual preceding date. It is scarce. There are twenty-five years in this series to '93. As the coinage of most of the O Mint dates was very large, they are easily obtained in some condition, except the 1852 scarce piece and the two superlative rarities we have referred to, which give this series its greatest interest to the numismatist. The Half Dollar of 1861 and the Double Eagle of the same date, were the only denominations coined that year at New Orleans on the eve of the war, all the other issues having ceased with the preceding date. It has been said that the major part of the large quantity of these Half

Dollars existing were coined with the remaining U. S. dies by the Confederacy in their pressing need of silver. We have heard this denied at the New Orleans Mint. At all events the coins cannot decide the matter or the different issues would have a greater interest.

THE S MINT HALF DOLLAR COINAGE

Is one of the most attractive series of all the Branch Mint issues. The Mint Mark has a greater number of sizes than in any other. There are a greater number of varieties than any except the Half Dime, and the Half Dollar has, from its size, an advantage over the latter in being seen in every detail without the use of a magnifying glass.

The conspicuous character of the largest S of the early San Francisco dates is thus even more notable on the Halves than the Quarters of this Mintage. It is quite as large or a little larger than the S's of the word 'STATES.' There is next a modified large S with a shorter upper curve. Then a medium s, a small s, and a very small s which occupies no more space than one of the periods on the piece. With a glass further distinctions might be made, but these will suffice for practical use. 1855 is the first year of the S Mint series. The date is large with far sloping 5's and with arrow heads. The Mint Mark is a large S placed close to the stem over the F of 'HALF.' This piece, though the reported coinage hardly warrants it, has become very rare, either from small issue perhaps or export. 1856 is without arrows, as are all afterwards down to '73, the date is large, with an upright 5 The large S is located as in '55. The 1857 has two varieties, a large S placed as in the preceding dates and a medium s high over the space between the F and D. Both varieties are very scarce and the latter may be called rare. The date continues large. 1858 presents the last large date and has two varieties, a large S high over the F and a medium s mid-high rather over the right of F. In 1859 the long continued medium date begins. The piece has two varieties, a large S high over the F, rather to the right and a medium s high, directly over the F. 1860 shows a large S high over the F, and a nearly as large S, but with a shorter upper curve, similarly placed on a second variety. 1861 offers two varieties also, a large S located as before and a medium s not so high over the F. In 1862 these varieties are repeated, but the medium s is rather smaller than the preceding one. 1863 has the first small s which is placed high over the space to the *left* of the F. 1864 gives two varieties again, a large S nearly over the space to the right of the F and a small s over the space to the left. The large S ceases with this date for 1865 shows only a small s mid-high over the staff of the F. 1866 has two varieties of a new character, one with the preceding plain field over the eagle, which has no counterpart in any other mintage of this date, and with a small s over the F, rather to the right; the second introducing on the field for all pieces thenceforward a scroll bearing the inscription 'In God We Trust.' This second has the small s over the space to the left of the F. 1867 has a small s high over the F. 1868 locates the same s high over the space to the left of the F. In 1869 the small s is just over the F and high. 1870 presents it over the F, but at lesser height. 1871 has two varieties, a small s moderately high, and a rather smaller s close to the stem, both over the F.

In 1872 two varieties are again found, one having a small s high over the F, the other placing it low over the space to the right. The 1873 date is accompanied by arrowheads, and has a small s close to the stem, over the space to the left of the F. 1874 continues the arrowheads, and has three varieties of slightly different small s's; one is very low over the space between F and D, the second is high over the F, and the third is high over the 'L' of 'HALF.' 1875 discontinues the arrowheads, and has also three varieties, a small s high over the F, another centered over the space to the right, and a very small s very close to the stem over the F. 1876 gives two varieties, one is a small s well centered over the F, the other a very small s placed as in the last date. In 1877 we have a small s high over the F, and, in a variety, the smallest sized s, well centered, over the F also.

All the pieces of this series, thus far, except 1855 and '57, should be readily found, but in the next date, 1878, we have the *great rarity* of the San Francisco Half Dollar coinage. It presents a very small s high over the F. After its very small coinage there was a break in the issue of this denomination until 1892, when the new dies of a bust of Liberty and an heraldic eagle were used, as at Philadelphia and New Orleans. A very small s is placed in this piece at the lowest point of the eagle's tail and just over the D. There is a variety with the S slightly larger and well centered. No coinage is probable in 1893.

There are, including dates to 1892, twenty-five pieces in the S mint series, and at least fifteen varieties. As the Halves at San Francisco were coined in much greater quantity than the Quarters, and are less worn usually by circulation, the collector can hope to collect a set of the former in much higher average condition.

THE CC MINT COINAGE OF HALF DOLLARS

Is, unlike its series of Dimes and Quarters, an unbroken sequence of nine dates from 1870 to 1878. Unlike them, also, however, no year's coinage was so very small as to be extremely rare. Yet three dates may be called very scarce and one variety rare. 1870 is the first of these dates. It has a pair of small upright cc's, close togther, and high over the F, rather to the left. 1871 and 1872 repeat these details. The former date, while not scarce, is certainly not common. 1873 presents two varieties. The first has a plain date, and the Mint Mark consists of two very small round cc's, close together, in the same location as before. This variety we consider rare. The second presents, for the first time, arrowheads at each side of the date, and has the upright, small, close cc's of preceding years. 1874 continues the arrowheads, and has the very small, close, rounded cc's high over the F, rather to the left. It is the second scarce date. 1875 discontinues the arrowheads, and offers two varieties. The first has the small upright cc's. but widely separated, in the usual location. The second shows the very small, rounded, close Mint Mark placed as before.

In 1876 we have again two varieties, small, close, upright cc's, rather to the left, over the F, and very small, rounded, close cc's directly over this letter. 1877 extends its varieties to three. The first is a very small, rounded, close pair of cc's high over the F and space to the right; the second a wider separated pair of upright small cc's high over the F, and to the left; the third gives the latter Mint Mark placed lower over the F. 1878 is the third scarce date of the series. Its Mint Mark, placed over the space to the left of the F, is the small upright pair of cc's in two varieties, one having the cc's even, the other having the first c higher than the second. Varieties thus extend the Carson City Half Dollar set to fifteen pieces.

THE SILVER DOLLAR,

Which has been such a cause of financial agitation of late years, and of which so many millions have been coined annually since 1878 not only at Philadelphia, but at each one of the Branch Mints of New Orleans, San Francisco and Carson City, seems, at first thought, too bulky, common and cumbrous a coin for the Mint Mark collector. To include dollars he must add, after a few early dates, three pieces each year from 1878 to the present to his Philadelphia series. But if he is an enthusiast in Mint Marks, he cannot omit the final silver series, especially if so easily acquired, for, as dollars have less wear than other denominations, he, if not willing to buy very fine or uncirculated specimens from the dealers, can find many dates of choice condition at the nearest bank. They will at any time realize more than third or fourth-rate coins of low intrinsic worth for which they might be spent. Interest only will be lost and, as mint mark coinage decreases and its collectors increase, even the dollars of desirable condition will surely yet command a good premium. And futhermore, despite the immense quantities of the majority of dates coined, there are certain rare pieces in the early issues of every Branch Mint which a numismatist may be very proud to possess.

THE O MINT SILVER DOLLAR COINAGE

Commenced with the year 1846, when the seated figure of Liberty appeared on the obverse, as in the Philadelphia issue. The Mint Mark is of the size of the usual O on the quarter and may be called large. It is well centered over the space between 'one' and 'dollar.' The piece is quite scarce. 1850 is the next year of coinage. The large O is high over the space. This dollar is *very* scarce—the most so of the series.

After another lapse of time the third O Mint Dollar was coined in 1859. A large O is moderately high over the space. The fourth coinage comes promptly in 1860 when the O is very high. This date and the preceding are scarce.

Then a long break occurs, commenced by the war and continued because no Trade Dollars were struck at New Orleans from 1873 to 1878 as at San Francisco and Carson City. When in 1879 O Mint Dollars were again coined—a year later than the Standard Dollar resumption at the San Francisco and Carson City mints—the large ornate head had replaced the seated figure of Liberty and, on the reverse, a different design is also seen. The Mint Mark changes to a small o which is close to the center of the wreath and over the space between the D and O of 'DOLLAR.' In the dates from 1879 to '93, the only variations from this description, which we have noted, are that the same small o sometimes touches the wreath, as in examples of 1886, 1888 and 1889, and sometimes is free. The date is also a little more or less removed from the star to the right. Such trifling differences would, we think, tempt no one to gather varieties of so inconvenient a piece, and we leave them undetailed.

THE S MINT SILVER DOLLAR COINAGE

Is irregular in the earlier dates, like the New Orleans series, and they are also much more limited in amount.

In 1859 the first San Francisco Dollars were coined with the 'Liberty seated' die. The s is nearly two-thirds of the size of the letters of 'STATES' and is high over the space between 'ONE' and 'DOLLAR'. The piece is rare. Not until 1872 was the next coinage of Dollars and it was so small as to make them very rare. The mint mark on our piece is a very small s that touches the stem directly over the E of 'ONE'. In the following year, 1873, but a few hundred pieces were struck which, in comparison with the few thousands of preceding dates and the many millions of those following, causes it to be excessively rare. As we have not yet seen or heard of a specimen we cannot give its discription, but if any one is lucky enough to find an 1873 S this will be unnecessary. The small coinage of this standard Dollar was probably due to the making of 700,000 of the Trade Dollars which was accomplished at San Francisco the same year.

THE S MINT TRADE DOLLARS.

1873, on the obverse of which is Liberty seated upon a bale with other details, has as Mint Mark a *very* small s over the D slightly to the left. 1874 has a small s in a similar position. 1875 offers two varieties, a very small and a medium sized s placed as before, but rather more to the left of D. 1876 has a medium s in the same location. In 1877 there is no change of Mint Mark, but, in addition to the regular piece, there is a curious variety resulting from the slipping of the 'collar' in the process of coinage. This gives an edge milled through half its thickness only, the rest being plain. The variety is known as the 1877 S mint half-milled dollar, and is rare. 1878 has the same rare variety. The regular piece has the S more nearly over the D. After 1873 the Trade Dollars were coined by millions annually, and no date should ordinarily be rare, but owing to export and the recall of about the entire amount of Trade Dollars once in circulation, few really exist out of dealers' and collectors' hands.

THE S MINT STANDARD DOLLARS—*Continued.*

In 1878, the last year of the coinage of Trade Dollars at San Francisco, the mint of that city resumed the issue of the more legitimate Dollar with an over-large and an over-ornate female head on the obverse. The Mint Mark on the reverse is a *very* small s over the space between the D and O of 'DOLLAR.' In 1879 the s is small and similarly placed. 1880 has a small crooked s. 1881 has a very small s once more and 1882 continues it. From 1883 on, a small s is seen in the same place until 1892, when a very small s returns. But the differences are, as in the O series, too slight for consideration in regard to this heavy piece of such immense annual coinage. 1893 has a small s.

The only dates in which somewhat less than a million were struck are 1886, 1888 and 1889, but condition alone can give value to any dollar of the S mint from 1878 to '93. It may be noted that the new designs of the Dimes, Quarters and Halves of 1892 were not extended to the Dollars, which in 1893 still appear as in the eighties at all mints.

THE CC MINT SILVER DOLLAR COINAGE,

Like that of the O and S institutions, presents its rarities early to the collector but they are in more regular order.

1870 was the first date of the Carson City Dollar. The piece has on its obverse the seated Liberty so long used. We have two varieties of this Mint Mark. In one the medium-sized, widely separated C C's are located high over the E and the space to the right; in the other the CC's are close together in the same position. Both varieties are very rare as but a few thousands were struck and they are very little known.

In 1871, 1872 and 1873 about two thousand Dollars only were coined annually at Carson City, and they are now extremely rare. The rarest 1871 has a large C C, rather wide, the first C over the E, the second touching the stem. 1872 we have not seen. The 1873 has the c c's of medium size and quite separated, one being over the E and the other over the space. We attribute the small coinage of Standard Dollars in Carson City, as at San Francisco, to the output of a very large amount of Trade Dollars in 1873, with a similar diversion of labor to them for several years to come.

THE CC MINT TRADE DOLLARS

Were issued contemporaneously with those of the S Mint during the years from 1873 to '78 inclusive. Though coined in smaller quantities the amount in circulation before the recall of the piece was not limited enough in any date to cause even scarcity. But if those remaining in the possession of collectors and dealers are proportioned relatively to the original coinage, the date of 1878 should be the most difficult to find.

The Trade Dollar 1873 c c has a medium sized, widely separated Mint Mark over the space before the D and the D itself. 1874 shows a small close pair of cc's in the same position. In 1875 the cc's are medium in size and close together over the space. 1876 has the medium and close cc's over the space and the D. 1877 repeats these details. 1878 offers the largest CC of all. The letters are close together and are over the D and the space to the right.

THE CC MINT STANDARD DOLLARS—*Continued.*

The new design of a large ornate head adopted for all the Mints, was used at Carson City in 1878 for a very large coinage of dollars with an individual value approximating those struck before 1873. The piece of 1878 has a small cc over the space between the D and O of 'DOLLAR.' In 1879 the same Mint Mark is more over the D. 1880 has a very small cc over the D and the space to the right. It is not very common. 1881 is becoming rather scarce. 1885 is quite scarce and 1889 moderately so. 1893 has a medium cc over the space between D and O. The first C is higher than the second. However, in the Carson Dollars from 1878 to '93 the differences are so trivial that, for reasons before given, we will leave further study of the millions of pieces annually issued to individual pleasure, assured that very few will burden their drawers with more than a specimen of each Mint Mark date.

Condition, we repeat, is an especially important factor of value in Dollars of the Branch Mints, and uncirculated pieces of the many abundant dates will command good premiums. Any prominent dealer could soon fill an order for one hundred strictly uncirculated Philadelphia coins of any silver denomination and date (except very few) between 1840 and 1890, but would find an equal number of any Branch Mint piece very difficult to gather in the same condition.

We have in these lists inserted the Trade Dollars in their regular order in the Branch Mint Coinage to better show their relation to the Standard Dollars and their occupation of the break in the series of that piece. But as many collectors keep their Trade Dollar set apart, we will show, in a mention of our array of these pieces, how an interest in Mint Marks may help to greatly enrich it.

To the eleven Philadelphia Proofs from 1873 to '83 may be added the five uncirculated dates from 1873 to '77 of the same Mint, the six regular Trade Patterns, the six S Mints from 1873 to '78, the six CC Mints of similar dates and the two Half Milled S Mints of 1877 and '78, making a collection of thirty-six pieces in all.

As another instance of how a study of Mint Marks will enable the numismatist to enrich his collection, we draw attention to the fact that there are no less than six different Silver Dollars of 1873 and 1878, as follows: The standard pieces of the Philadelphia, the Carson City, and the San Francisco Mints, together with the 'Trades' of the Carson City and San Francisco Mints, make five pieces for each date, and for the sixth the '73 P Mint can be had, both uncirculated and in proof, and the '78 P in proof only, with seven and with eight tail feathers to the eagle.

There is also a rare 1878 dollar, which has three single leaves on the stem in the eagle's claw instead of the usual three groups of three leaves each, and which, being otherwise, obverse and reverse, exactly like the standard P mint 1878, does not deserve to be called a 'pattern.' But we are wandering somewhat, in our remarks upon general varieties, from the subject of Mint Marks to which this Treatise is devoted. A study of them in every silver series has, however, now been completed.

The years of issue at the Branch Mints of each denomination from the Three Cent piece to the Dollar have been carefully given, and all varieties thus far discovered particularly mentioned, both to show what are known to exist and to stimulate a search for others which may yet be found, a search not only for varieties, but for Mint Mark rare dates hitherto overlooked which any one may retrieve from circulation and dispose of at a high price.

BRANCH MINT RARITIES.

The leading coins thus referred to are here compactly given:

Silver Dollars, CC, 1870, '71, 72, '73; S, 1859, '72, '73; O, 1846, '50.

Half Dollars, O, 1838, '53, no arrows or rays; S, 1855, '57, '78; CC, '73, no arrows.

Quarters, CC, 1870, '71, '72, '73; S, '64, '66, '71.

Twenty Cent piece, CC, '76.

Dimes, CC, 1871, '72, '73, '74; O, '60; S, '58, '59, '70, '85.

Half Dimes, O, 1838, '42, '44, '48, '49, '52; S, '71.

These pieces range from rare to extremely rare. Many merely scarce ones are not added that those of the first importance may be more clearly kept in mind.

POSSIBILITIES.

We have never heard of the following varieties in standard coin, but they may exist: Half Dollar, 1873, S, without arrows; Quarters, '53, O, no arrows and rays; '66, S, no motto;

'73, S, no arrows; Dimes, '53, O, no arrows; '40, O, with sleeve; '73, S, without arrows.

EXCLUSIVE MINT MARKS.

It has already been mentioned that several dies were used at the Branch Mints which were either never employed at Philadelphia or not during the same year. The resultant coins have a peculiar interest, and are here assembled, being not patterns, but standard pieces:

The Half Dime of 1838, O, without stars.

The Dime of 1838, O, without stars.

The Dime of 1860, S, with stars.

The Quarter of 1840, O, without sleeve.

The Half Dollar of 1853, O, without arrows and rays.

The Half Dollar of 1866, S, without the motto 'In God we Trust.'

The Half Dime and Dime without stars were issued in 1837 at Philadelphia, but not in '38. The last Philadelphia Dime with stars was struck in 1859. The other pieces have been referred to in past pages.

UNAPPRECIATED PHILADELPHIA RARITIES.

As a matter of interesting comparison we will follow the list of pieces which are rare as 'Mint Marks,' but not so as Philadelphia coinage, with a list of those considered rare in any case by dealers and collectors, and which are really much rarer in the Philadelphia than the Branch Mint issues.

Half Dimes, 1863, '64, '65, '66, and '67, but *especially* the '64, are high rarities if without an 'S' upon them. In the San Francisco Mint the coinage averaged nearly $6,000 worth annually. In Philadelphia about $500, and of the 1864 date but $23.50. Dimes, 1866 and '67, of Philadelphia have not a fifteenth of the issue of the S mint. Quarters, 1841 and '42, are still rarer without the O, '42 *especially*, and 1866, '67, '68, and '69 without the S. 1888 is very common with the S and very rare without it.

These points illustrate the advantage of a knowledge of Mint Marks even to those who do not collect them.

Half Dollars, though several immense S Mint issues surpass greatly several large issues of similar date at Philadelphia, offer but one notable greater rarity in the latter coinage, that of 1852.

In Dollars the date 1850 of Philadelphia is much rarer than the O Mint piece, the coinage being but a fifth of the latter.

Trade Dollars of the Philadelphia Mint are in a decided minority compared with others in the years 1874 and '75 only, but, as we have before said, the almost entire remelting of the 'Trades' nullifies all influence of issue.

Philadelphia scarce dates have not been here referred to except in comparison with competitive Branch Mint pieces. The rare ones coined in Philadelphia only, are beyond our province of reference.

MINT MARK SETS.

We have thus far spoken of Mint Marks rather as associated with Philadelphia contemporary dates, than as independent series. But there is no need of inserting them among the pieces of the older Mint. Kept by themselves the irregularities of issue are better fixed on the mind, and the differences in the distinguishing letters and in other peculiarities are more apparent.

Mint Marks can be classified either according to the various Mints or by denominations, and a collector cannot realize fully, until he sees the many dates and varieties of any mintage so arranged, how interesting and valuable they are. A beginner may indeed commence with Mint Marks only. He will thus postpone the outlay involved in gathering the older and rarer Philadelphia coinage, he will find a much larger proportion of needed pieces in circulation, he will discover occasional varieties, now rarely possible in old coin, and he will accumulate series of modern pieces in desirable condition which will have high value in the future.

UNITED STATES GOLD MINT MARKS.

The collector of United States gold coins has two difficulties to contend with. First, owing to the general preference for 'greenbacks,' gold is far less circulated in our country, except in the extreme West, than is similar coinage among other nations. Secondly, the much larger export of gold than of silver coin tends to greatly increase the scarcity of remote issues. These difficulties relate, of course, to the Branch Mint coinages as much as to that of Philadelphia, and they are all inextricably confused. Many fine gold collections exist, however, for, in proportion to face value, such coin is cheaper than silver or copper, but in collections of gold the mintage is disregarded.

We have heard of no collector who, except in the gold Dollar series, has attempted to confine his pieces to one mint, and have had no opportunity to verify the gold coinage of the Mint Report as we have done in silver. Yet in the mixed pieces of any set, Mint Marks are frequent enough to suggest the general correctness of the Report and to prompt a new ambition.

Certain gold coins have a uniformly larger issue of dates at some one Branch Mint than at all others, and if collectors or numismatic associations in New Orleans, San Francisco, Carson City, Charlotte and Dahlonega, or their vicinity, who have access to bank deposits, should begin to collect sets of the mintage in their sections, as well as chance scarce pieces of others, and should establish correspondence and exchange, one might soon hear of far advanced gold Mint Mark collections which would be an honor to the enterprising numismatists possessing them.

The Gold coin hunter will find the trail in the following pages devoted to different mintages in detail.

THE GOLD DOLLAR.

Since the suspension of the gold Dollar coinage in 1889, the piece has been much used for ornament and, regardless of date or condition, now commands nearly fifty cents premium. It has attracted great attention from many collectors who have sought no other gold series, and its Mint Marks have become generally very rare. They number thirty-five in all.

The New Orleans or O issue has six dates as follows: 1849, '50, '51, '52, '53 and '55. The 1850 only is rare.

The precious Dahlonega or 'D' mint issues are thirteen, of the years 1849, '50, '51, '52, '53, '54, '55, '56, '57, '58, '59, '60 and '61. Of these 1852 and '53 are rare; 1854, '57 and '58 are very rare; 1860, exceedingly rare; 1855 and '56, excessively rare, and of 1861, which is not in the Mint Report, but two pieces are known, one being in our possession.

The Charlotte or 'C' mint issues are nine—1849, '50, '51, '52, '53, ('54), '55, '57 and '59. Of these, 1859, '50, '52 and '55 range from very rare to rare, and '54 is not to be considered attainable as, according to the Report, but four pieces were coined and these are now unknown.

The 'S' or San Francisco issues are seven—1854, '56, '57, '58, '59, '60 and '70, all being obtainable but the latter, which is excessively rare and the only one of the gold Dollar Mint Marks that we do not possess.

The following details will be of interest regarding the mintages named: The '49 O has a small planchet, small o and open wreath (at top). The '50 O has a small planchet, small o, slanting 5 and close wreath. '51, '52 and '53 are similar, but with a large 'O,' and '55 has a slanting 5, close wreath and large O on a large planchet.

The '49 D and the '50 and '51 have small planchets and small D's, the '49 an open wreath, and the others a slanting 5. The '52, '53 and '54 have small planchets and close wreaths, but the '52 and '53 have a large D, and the '54 a small one. 1855 D has a large planchet and a small D, a slanting 5 and a close wreath. 1856 D has a large planchet, a large D, an upright 5 and a close wreath, as have all the following (except as regards the absent 5 in '60 and '61). The latter two dates are much smaller than the others.

The 49 C has a small planchet, a small c and a *close wreath*, thus differing from the two other mintages of this date, the Philadelphia Dollar of 1849 having both varieties. '50 and '51 C are similar to '49 C, and with a slanting 5. 1852 and '53 C are similar, except in having a large C. 1855 C has a large planchet and a small c with close wreath and slanting 5 as before. 1857 and '59 have a large planchet, a large C, an upright 5 and the wreath continuing close.

The 1854 S has a small planchet, a large S, a slanting 5 and a close wreath. There was no coinage in 1855 at the Charlotte Mint. The '56 and following S dates have a large planchet and S, an upright 5 and the wreath close as usual. The 1860 S has a smaller date than the others.

All the gold Dollars present, on the obverse, a woman's head of classic character on the *small planchet* and an Indian girl's head with a plumed coronet on the *large*. There are two sizes of the Indian head. The smaller size of the Philadelphia date of 1855 is also seen on the O, C and D mintages of the same date and on the S mintage of 1856. All other large planchet dates have the larger Indian head.

THE THREE DOLLAR PIECE,

A beautiful coin abolished with the Gold Dollar in 1889, has the same Indian head of larger size than the Dollars throughout the series. Its few Mint Marks will consequently be next mentioned. In 1854 only (the year of its first issue in Philadelphia,) the piece was coined at the New Orleans and Dahlonega Mints—the latter Mark being very rare and the O common. But at San Francisco there were issues in 1855, '56, '57 and '60. All are very rare except the 1856, which, however, is interesting from having two varieties, a large and a small S.

With these our direct knowledge of Mint Mark *varieties* in the precious metal ceases, as we have found no gold collectors who notice them, and as our collection in bank has no other gold than the One Dollar and Three Dollar series (these being complete in all Mints, except one piece). We can, however, give the Branch Mint dates and rarities of the '*Eagle Denominations*,' until their varieties come to light.

THE QUARTER EAGLE ($2.50)

Was coined at the New Orleans Mint in the years from 1839 to '57, except 1844, '45, '48, '49, '53 and '55. The rarest date is 1841 and 1842, '39, '56, '40 and '57 are scarce.

The Dahlonega issue is from 1839 to '59, except 1858 only. None are common and the following dates are very rare, 1856, '55, '54, '59, '57, '53 and '40—the rarest date being given first and the others in order.

The Charlotte issue is from 1838 to '60, except the years 1845, '53, '57 and '59. The rare date is '55, followed by '46 '42 and '60 at greater distance.

The San Francisco issue is from 1854 to '79, except '55, '64 and '74. The great prize of the series is 1858. 1876 is scarce, but no other date should be so from the amount coined.

This ends the Quarter Eagle Mint Marks, as the coin has never been issued at Carson City. There are seventy-five in number to 1893, representing $187.50 in face value

THE HALF EAGLE ($5.00)

Was coined in New Orleans from 1840 to '57 except 1848, '49, '50, '52 and '53. No date should be even very scarce in the South, but '41 more nearly so.

Dahlonega issued the piece from 1838 to '61 consecutively. The last date is *very* rare.

The Charlotte issue was during the same period, except in the year 1845. Of the C dates, 1861 is scarcest, with '46, '60 and '40 in order.

The San Francisco list extends from 1854 to '88. Its first issue, '54, is exceedingly rare and should command a high price. 1864 and '76 are rare, '75 and '62 scarce. The rest should be readily found in the far western banks. Carson City issued Half Eagles from 1870 to '84 continuously. No date is of small issue and all may be hopefully sought where western gold circulates.

The number of Half Eagle Mint Marks to 1893 is 115, representing $575.00 in face value.

THE EAGLE OR $10 PIECE.

This was coined in New Orleans from 1841 to '61, from '79 to '83, and also in '88. The date 1883 is a high prize. 1879 is very rare, '59 and '41 are rare and '57 scarce. With these gained, one might be sure of the rest at leisure.

No Eagles were coined at Dahlonega or Charlotte—a great saving of time and money to the collector.

The coinage at San Francisco is from 1854 to the present, except 1875. There are no very small issues, but pieces of '64 must be very scarce and '60, '76, '69, '59, '70, '55 and '67 follow in moderating importance.

In Carson City Eagles were coined from 1870 to '84 continuously. 1879 is rare, 1878, '77, '73 and '76 are more or less scarce and chances favor the finding of the other dates where CC issues are much seen.

The total Eagle Mint Marks to '93 number 80, or a face value of $800.

DOUBLE EAGLES OR $20 PIECES.

In New Orleans Double Eagles were coined from 1850 to '61 and not again until 1879. 1856, '79 and '54 are very scarce dates. The others should be freely found. The San Francisco Mint has issued this coin from 1854 to the present (except the void year 1886), in such uniformly large amounts that the smallest coinage in 1887 is of 283,000 pieces. All should be common by this criterion.

Neither at Dahlonega or Charlotte was the Double Eagle coined, a fact which aspiring gold collectors will be relieved to know.

Carson City supplies the piece from 1870 to '85 (except in 1881 and '82), and from 1889 to the present date of '93. The first date only should be rare and 1885, '79, '78 and '81 rather scarce.

There are in all seventy-one Double Eagle Mint Marks to 1893, representing a face value of $1,420.

The total value of all denominations of Gold Mint Marks to the same year is a little short of $3,050.

While the majority of collectors engaged with the older Philadelphia coinage in all metals, might not desire to carry this additional sum, it is far less than the more advanced among them have spent in that direction for pieces that would not average in intrinsic value a fifth of the amount named.

As the premiums upon gold coin are relatively much lower than on any other, a collection of gold Mint Marks would be not only a very interesting pursuit to the wealthy numismatist or to any prominent institution, but would prove neither extravagant or unprofitable, for such a collection would be a distinguishing possession and if bought prudently, would sell, if necessary, much closer to its cost than many miscellaneous collections of silver and copper which are thrown upon the market.

Collectors should, at all events, if living near any one of the Branch Mints, seek to gather a series of one or more of its gold denominations. They should without fail, save the rarest dates of any series if chancing upon them, for with the decline of Mint Mark coinage, such pieces will attain very great value.

These rarest pieces of Branch Mint Gold Coinage we assemble on the following page in the order of Date but not of value, to be better remembered.

INDIAN HEAD SERIES.

Gold Dollars.—O 1850: D '52, '53, '54, '55, '56, '57, '58, '60 and '61: C, 50, '52, '54, '55, '59: S 1870.

Three Dollars.—D 1854: S '55, '57, '60.

EAGLE SERIES.

Quarter Eagles, $2.50.—O 1841: D 1840, '53, '54, '55, '56, '57 and '59: C 1855: S 1858.

Half Eagles.—D 1861: S 1854, '64, '76.

Eagles.—O 1883, '79, '59, '41: S 1864: CC 1879.

Double Eagles.—O 1854, '56 and '79: CC 1890.

There are a few more or less scarce dates in each series which have been already noted and are not included here that the rare pieces may be clearly distinguished.

From the very limited use of gold in the greater part of the United States, these pieces are not to be found by simply waiting for them to appear in circulation as in the case of silver coin, nor will they form part of the collections that revert to dealers for sale. It becomes therefore of the utmost importance that dealers and collectors should use all influence to examine the gold reserve of the banks in their vicinity, or that paying tellers, and those persons who count the cash in Government vaults, Sub-Treasuries, Branch Mints and private financial institutions, should be somewhat informed numismatically, both for their own profit and the enriching of private and public collections by their discoveries. But it would cause less delay hêre also if some experienced collector were authorized to be present when the counting of coin was in progress, both to see the contents of sacks and to mark upon them as far as possible the period of the coinage they contained.

Furnished with a number of pieces of the denominations undergoing count, his trained eye could quickly detect rarities which he could at once secure and replace.

HISTORY IN MINT MARKS.

Among the attractions of Branch Mint coin collecting, we have referred to the connection these pieces have with national progress and the financial conditions of the country. This feature ever gives to Numismatics its highest dignity and in no coinage destitute of portraits can history be so well read 'between the lines' as in that of the several Mints of the United States. With the establishment in 1838 of those at New Orleans, Dahlonega and Charlotte, we mark the rapid prosperity of the South from its rich products and growing commerce. Until toward 1840, the country at large and the South especially had been flooded with Spanish coins. But these were banished from circulation by law and from the first modest coinage of Dimes and Half Dimes at New Orleans in 1838, that mint rapidly enlarged its issues, especially in the Half Dollars, until local demands were well supplied with many millions of O Mint silver.

Few Silver Dollars were coined, as State Banks issued bills of this value in sufficient quantity.

The gold coinage of New Orleans commenced soon after the silver, with Quarter Eagles, Half Eagles and Eagles, the issues of the former and latter rapidly increasing in amount. In the few years from 1850, millions of Double Eagles were added to Southern wealth, and a quantity of Gold Dollars. Then the entire O Mint coinage gradually diminished until the Civil War in 1861 caused a long interruption. From 1879 millions of Silver Dollars and a moderate number of Eagles coined at New Orleans testify to the South's more substantial recuperation. Within two or three years all denominations of Silver and several of Gold have again been issued from the O Mint, but owing to the early construction of a much larger mint at Philadelphia, the prospects are that any great coinage at New Orleans has about come to an end, unless political influence overrules national economy of production.

The Mints at Dahlonega and Charlotte coined only gold Quarter Eagles, Half Eagles, Three Dollar and One Dollar pieces. The Three Dollar piece appeared in small quantity in 1854 only at the D Mint. Small issues of the Dollars were made by both Mints from 1849 to '60, but the Eagle denominations mentioned, especially the Half Eagles, were struck annually in large numbers as a division of patronage with New Orleans, and give a total Southern coinage of gold quite indicative of the affluence of that section during the period in which it was supplied.

The great West was meanwhile growing in population and material wealth with amazing rapidity. Its mixed races, natural advantages and invigorating atmosphere developed the highest activity and commercial progress. When the discovery of the precious metals in California and Nevada made the West in 1849 an Eldorado of the world, its financial needs commanded recognition and its remote mines and population a place of coinage adjacent to them.

The San Francisco mint was accordingly established in 1854. Its very commencement shows the boundless resource, confidence and energy of the section in which it was located. It plunged into the higher denominations of gold coinage at once and soon took the lion's share of the burden from Philadelphia.

The first issues were nearly three million dollars worth of Double Eagles and over a million worth of Eagles. And though other gold and silver denominations were soon very regularly coined they were but in moderate or small quantity. For nearly forty years an average of from fifteen to twenty million dollars worth of Double Eagles have been annually struck in San Francisco. This magnificence of wealth makes the more neglected denominations quite rare and therefore more desirable to the Numismatist, as his main wish to possess the larger S mint pieces would be in order to spend them for the smaller ones. Very few gold or silver dollars were coined in San Francisco until 1873 and, of other silver, only the Half Dollars in more than small or moderate quantity, although the civil war caused a long interruption to issues from Southern Mints and threw a greater burden upon the Philadelphia and Western production.

Yet California has never seen the day of small things or of small coin in any quantity and its dates of high intrinsic value are far easier to collect than the small, while in the East the contrary is the case. When mining interests began to affect national legislation and the dishonest Trade Dollar was authorized, the San Francisco Mint, as convenient to silver mines and Chinese commerce, plunged again into restless coinage with an issue of four or five millions of these pieces annually from 1873 to '78. From 1875 to '77 there was a flood of Halves, Quarters and Dimes also. Then it gave its energies to a yearly average of about eight million of the standard Dollars and all other pieces than gold Double Eagles have since been practically disdained.

Thus all the indications of San Francisco coinage point to opulence and a lavish use of money, with the prospect of long-assured prosperity.

The Carson City Mint was organized to share with San Francisco something of the burden of coinage which rich mines, rapid growth and the civil war transferred so largely to the West. It was active from 1870—the starting year—to 1885 in the coinage of gold, and followed the S Mint in a much larger issue of Double Eagles than of other pieces; but from 1870 to '78 it issued all current denominations of gold and silver in a fair relative proportion and in a peculiarly regular and moderate annual amount. It seemed rather to be doing a general service in a uniform way than supplying irregular needs of the section in which it was located. In 1878 its silver coinage was abruptly stopped in every denomination, owing probably to the immense issues of subsidiary coin at Philadelphia for the few preceding years, and in 1885 its coinage of gold yielded to other Mints also. Since that date the Carson City Mint has coined Double Eagles and Silver Dollars only. While it thus receives little present attention, its small coinage of many series for eight years the past will always attract the great interest of collectors. The future of the San Francisco and Carson City Mints, as affected by the greatly to be increased coinage capacity of that at Philadelphia, cannot be foretold, but it seems as if their distance from the East and nearness to the mines would, apart from any sectional support, prolong their usefulness.

These brief evidences of the illustration of American events in the Mint Mark coinage can be followed up with increasing interest by a closer study of the Mint Report's tables of annual issues. This, however, would only begin the subject. Any elderly Mint officer or financier who has considered the monetary questions of the United States for the past fifty years could, no doubt, supply enough additional facts connected with the coinage of the Branch Mints to make in themselves a volume of historic interest.

But, in suggesting the range and dignity of the topic, our purpose here is sufficiently accomplished, and we leave to others a study of the effects upon the Branch Mint issues of prosperous and disastrous commercial periods, greater or less product of mines, wise or imprudent legislation, large or small export of gold and silver, relative sectional progress and influence and the varying distribution of coinage between the Philadelphia Mint and its distant associates.

NOTE.—It should be stated, that while the dates of all denominations of coins at the Branch Mints are rarely entirely consecutive, the Philadelphia Mint has since 1838 coined every authorized denomination of gold and silver money annually (however small the coinage of some years) except the Quarter Eagle of 1841.

CONCLUSION.

In a final word we urge upon all American numismatists the giving of their attention to the Branch Mint coinage of our country without delay. If not to all, certainly to the silver series.

A few collectors are already on the alert. Since commencing to write this Treatise we have heard of large purchases of choice Branch Mint gold at Southern and Western banks, of the accumulation of hundreds of uncirculated Silver Mint Marks of late dates by prominent dealers with a view to future demand, and of many things which prove that this pursuit is not the fancy of the few or of the moment, but is the vigorous beginning of a permanently established department of numismatic science. This activity is none too soon.

Circulating money contains many prizes in this new branch of coin study which any one may find, which each week's wear will injure in condition and which some early year's remelting may remove forever.

Dealers have an opportunity in Mint Marks, which catalogues show they are beginning to perceive, of doubling tripling or, at times, even quadrupling their sales of pieces from 1838 to the present. Collectors in different sections of the Union have, in the coins therein produced, an unequaled cause of active correspondence and profitable exchange, and the whole numismatic world possesses, as this Treatise has fully shown, substantial reason for new and zealous interest in modern United States Coinage.

ERRATA.

Page 3.—Carson Mint, second line, substitute 'and' for 'as were.'

Page 8—latter half.—'Philatalist' should be Philatelist.

Page 18.—'Half Dimes of '37' should be Half Dime of '37; and, under 'S Mint Half Dimes, '84 and '83' should be '64 and '63.

Page 21.—26th line substitute 'from '92' for 'of this date.'

Page 28.—S Mint Quarters. In first paragraph the word 'Quarters' should be inserted after '90.

N. B.—The 1893 S Quarter, just received, has a small s under the right side of the tail and over the space between R and D.

www.ingramcontent.com/pod-product-compliance
Lightning Source LLC
Chambersburg PA
CBHW021640270326
41931CB00008B/1102

9783337340810